12 Steps to
Self - Improvement

12 Steps to Self - Improvement

An Assessment Profile

EDITED BY

Michael Crisp

**KOGAN
PAGE**

First published in the United States of America
in 1991 by Crisp Publications Inc, 95 First Street,
Los Altos, California 94022, USA.

This edition first published in Great Britain in
1992 by Kogan Page Ltd, 120 Pentonville Road,
London N1 9JN.

British Library Cataloguing in Publication Data

A CIP record for this book is available from the British Library.

ISBN 0-7494-0611-9

Typeset by DP Photosetting, Aylesbury, Bucks
Printed and bound in Great Britain by
Biddles Ltd, Guildford and Kings Lynn

Contents

Introduction

When times get tough, it is easy for a person to lose his or her enthusiasm and turn negative. Such down periods are accelerated when organisations are forced by external conditions such as domestic and international competition and/or a recession to tighten their belts. During these times, the survivors will need to get greater productivity from employees.

There is an expression, 'I'm going on holiday to sort things out.' All of us occasionally feel the need to get away and take a new look at our careers or our lives in general. Some of us take a short break to go through the process. Others can do it over a weekend at home. Still others 'sort things out' by taking a long drive in the country.

During these restoration periods, it is a good idea to view yourself as a battery that has started to lose its energy and needs a recharge. Consider this book as the 'recharge machine'. The self-improvement inventory (profile) you will be taking will measure how well you have charged your battery.

One other thought: why not forget the conditions that existed in the past and accept more demanding challenges that can also lead to success in the future?

It is the smart thing to do!

Michael G Crisp

PART 1
Profile Categories

> 'When the going gets tough, the tough get going.'
>
> *Cher (among others)*

CATEGORY 1
How High Is Your Self-esteem?

What is self-esteem?

Self-esteem is the way you perceive yourself. If you view yourself as inferior to others, or as having little confidence to do everyday things, you are lacking in self-esteem. If, on the other hand, you are full of confidence and consider yourself to be competent in most situations, you have good self-esteem. Those perceived as having high self-esteem are often chosen as leaders when presented with an opportunity.

Self-esteem translates into self-worth. When you place a high value on yourself as a person, you respect your skills and abilities and have confidence in what you can accomplish. If you have self-esteem, you do not back away from challenges. You are a professional!

Education can help to give people self-esteem. For example, those who have been to university often exhibit more self-worth than those who have not. *But not always.* Many people without higher education, through experience and self-improvement, demonstrate a greater degree of self-esteem than those with degrees.

Having a high degree of self-esteem usually gives one a comfortable, secure feeling inside that manifests itself in a positive, confident attitude. This is good news, but people who think well of themselves still need to be sensitive when building relationships with others.

Self-esteem is a precious commodity that needs to be balanced with a degree of humility.

Measure your self-esteem*

Mark a 'T' for true or 'F' for false before each statement as it normally relates to your thinking.

_____ 1. I feel my work/career has progressed more because of luck and not because I deserve it.

_____ 2. I often find myself thinking, 'Why can't I be more successful?'

_____ 3. I do not believe I am working to my full potential.

_____ 4. I consider it a failure when I do not accomplish my goals.

_____ 5. When others are nice to me I often feel suspicious.

_____ 6. Paying others compliments about their strengths often makes me feel uncomfortable.

_____ 7. It is difficult to see colleagues being promoted because I often feel I am more deserving.

_____ 8. I do not necessarily believe that my mind has a direct influence on my physical well-being.

_____ 9. When things are going well, they do not usually last for me.

_____ 10. I place a high value on what others think of me.

_____ 11. I like to impress my supervisor.

_____ 12. I find it difficult to face up to my mistakes.

_____ 13. I am not comfortable always saying what I mean.

_____ 14. I find it hard to say I am sorry.

_____ 15. I tend to accept change in my job slowly because of fear.

---

* This exercise is taken from the book _Developing Self-esteem_ By Connie Palladino, Kogan Page.

_____ 16. Procrastination is a good word to describe my work habits.

_____ 17. I often find myself thinking, 'Why even try, I won't make it?'

_____ 18. When my boss praises me, I usually do not believe him or her.

_____ 19. I do not think my colleagues want me to advance professionally.

_____ 20. I avoid people who I think do not like me.

_____ 21. My attitude towards life could improve.

_____ 22. If I am honest with myself, I tend to blame my parents for how my life is turning out.

_____ 23. I find it difficult to look for the good in others.

_____ 24. I do not think people can change their attitudes.

_____ 25. I really do not believe that a self-help book will make a difference to my self-esteem.

Add up all your TRUE and FALSE statements.

TRUE: _____ FALSE: _____

If you scored over half the items 'True', you may want to spend some time on your own or with a counsellor, thinking about your life. Think about why you have these feelings.

If the majority of your answers were 'False' you seem to have good self-esteem and are on your way to greater success and satisfaction.

On the following page you will find two cases. Study them carefully and then compare your thoughts with those of the author (page 93).

Case studies

1. Jill

Jill always seems to denigrate her abilities and appearance. For some reason she does not look as good to herself as she does to others. If Jill were to rate her self-image on a scale of 1 to 10, her rating would be 3 or 4.

Her low rating is partially due to the fact that Jill honestly believes her parents did not expect her to achieve as much as her older sister who was always a good student and class leader. Another reason is that Jill seldom sticks up for herself at work or during family situations. Rather than communicate her true feelings, she usually just walks away.

In her first job since leaving school, Jill is underemployed in view of her abilities and skills. If her self-esteem had been higher, management would have provided several promotional opportunities in the past three years.

If you had a close relationship with Jill how would you assist her to go about building her self-esteem to a higher level?

2. James

James is a highly respected and competent employee. He is a consistently high producer, seldom absent, and works well with fellow employees. James frequently works overtime because colleagues lean on him for help during regular office hours. He is conservative in his grooming.

James hopes to become a manager eventually, but he refuses to see himself as a leader. Although others might consider him to be a 'soft touch', he can, at times, take a firm stand on an important matter. A graduate, James is currently taking evening classes in preparation for an MBA.

On a scale of 1 to 10, James would rate himself about a 5 as far as self-esteem is concerned. He recognises that he needs to communicate a more positive and assertive image but, so far, he is content to remain as a likeable member of his work group.

Social acceptance is more important at this stage than a big career step upwards.

What suggestions would you make to James if he came to you for help in improving his self-esteem?

To compare your thoughts with those of the author, turn to page 93.

Self-inventory scale

It is now time for you to rate yourself on a specific scale. This scale will be used for all 12 categories covered in this book. Please follow carefully the instructions below.

On a scale of 1 to 10, rate your honest perception in the area of your *self-esteem*. Do this by circling the appropriate number on the scale below.

- If you circle 1, 2 or 3, you are saying you need *significant* improvement to reach your potential.
- If you circle 4, 5 or 6, you are recording that you need *considerable* improvement to reach your potential.
- Should you circle 8, 9 or 10, you are asserting that you need *little* or *no* improvement to reach your potential.

Please be honest with yourself. Keep in mind that the middle of the scale is average. Most people rate themselves somewhere in the middle of the scale. Take your time. It will be from ratings similar to this that you will build your individual profile on page 73 of the book.

Self-inventory scale
Self-esteem

Low									High
1	2	3	4	5	6	7	8	9	10

CATEGORY 2
Do You See the Wellness-Success Connection?

Wellness defined

The intriguing thing about wellness is that you tend to know when you enjoy it and when you don't. When you are well, there is normally a feeling of vitality and personal confidence. You feel in tune with your environment. Your energy is high. When unwell, you feel tired, draggy and down. Nothing seems right.

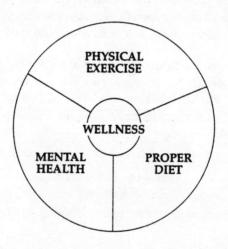

The above diagram illustrates three major contributing factors to wellness:

Physical exercise

Those who are involved in physical fitness know the benefits it brings. Regular exercisers understand that a person not only feels better following a workout but he or she is building a stronger body for the future.

Proper diet

Good nutrition is essential. In addition to giving your body the necessary vitamins and minerals, a proper diet helps to 'normalise' weight. Coordinating an exercise programme with a proper diet is the best of both worlds. It takes time, effort and sometimes help from an outside source to achieve consistent results.

Mental health

Although exercise and diet may be the primary sources of wellness, both need to be viewed from the perspective of mental health. Each supports the other, and it is the combination of all three that adds up to true wellness.

Wellness, then, is a holistic concept, saying that the sum (wellness) can be greater than all the contributing parts. When you weave all three elements into one fabric you have the foundation upon which to build your professional career. Without wellness your personal goals and dreams may never be achieved.

Wellness and the attitude connection

Apparently no one has been able to prove conclusively a clinical relationship between physical well-being and attitude. Most, however, including the most cynical of researchers in the area, concede there is a connection. Answer the following questions and compare your answers with those of the author overleaf.

True False

☐   ☐   1. Exercise can do more to adjust your attitude than a cocktail 'happy hour'.

☐ ☐ 2. Following a good diet has nothing to do with improving your self-image.

☐ ☐ 3. The better you feel physically on a given day, the more positive your attitude is apt to be.

☐ ☐ 4. Neither a sense of physical well-being nor a positive attitude can be stored indefinitely.

☐ ☐ 5. Daily exercise can do little to keep one positive.

Typical wellness comments

More than at any previous time in our history, there is public awareness of physical fitness. A surprising number of us incorporate daily workouts into our schedules. This commitment to the 'attitude connection' is expressed in these typical comments.

'My workout does as much for my mental state as it does for my body.'

'Exercise tones up my body and tunes up my outlook.'

'I never underestimate what my daily workout does for me psychologically.'

Many fitness enthusiasts depend on exercise to keep them out of attitudinal ruts.

'I've renamed my health club The Attitude Adjustment Factory.'

'When I'm worried or depressed, I take a long walk. It has a way of pushing negative thoughts out of my system.'

Author's answers
1. T (both will change your focus, but exercise is better for you and lasts longer); 2. F; 3. T; 4. T; 5. F (Daily exercise is an outstanding attitude adjuster.)

'A good workout can get me out of a mental rut.'

No single group in our society deals more with the psychological aspects of attitude than professional athletes. Increasingly, athletes engage year-round in sophisticated physical conditioning programmes. They realise they must stay in shape to remain competitive. If you listen carefully, coaches and managers talk more about attitude than physical conditioning.

'We made the play-offs this year because we have a new team attitude.'

'I owe my success this season to my coach. He helped me to adjust not only my technique, but more importantly, my attitude.'

'My success this year is due to greater self-confidence. I finally began to believe in myself.'

As important as talent and physical conditioning are, most players, coaches and sports commentators talk about mental attitude as most important.

They must be trying to tell us something.

Case studies

3. Gemma

Gemma is your favourite colleague. She has become a good friend. Gemma is efficient, effective, and builds excellent relationships both on the job and in her personal world, but she has an image problem due primarily to her excessive weight.

Gemma is always on a new weight-loss programme. When the diet is successful and she loses some weight, she becomes positive, productive and creative. But she always seems to abandon the programme after a while and regains the weight. When this happens, she becomes slightly negative and withdrawn and falls into a productivity slump.

Gemma knows the up-and-down pattern she follows and has come to you for guidance. What suggestions would you make?

4. Keith

Maggie is concerned about her husband for two reasons. First, whatever activity Keith goes into (running, cycling, surfing) he overdoes it and, as a result, suffers excessive exhaustion. Sometimes it takes him two or three days to get his full energy level back. Second, although it happens infrequently, he is so competitive that when he does well in an event he celebrates too much with his many friends and this further breaks down his energy level.

Maggie does not feel that Keith understands the true meaning of wellness, and she fears he is damaging his long-term health. She has used the term 'moderation' so often that using it further is meaningless.

How might Maggie protect Keith from his own excesses?

Turn to page 93 for the views of the author.

Self-inventory scale

It is now time for you to rate yourself on your state of wellness as it has existed during the past year. As you do this, consider the following factors:

- The kind of exercise regimen you have consistently practised.
- The nutrition programme you have followed throughout the year.
- Your use of tobacco, alcohol and drugs.
- Weight maintenance at the level you desire.
- The success you have had in managing stress.
- Your ability to relax and sleep normal hours.
- How well you have been able to 'balance your life'.

Do not give yourself a high rating unless you have earned it.

Self-inventory scale
Wellness

Low									High
1	2	3	4	5	6	7	8	9	10

CATEGORY 3
Are You a Good Communicator?

The art of communication

Hundreds of excellent books have been written about aspects of communication. Some publications place emphasis on interpersonal communication, others deal primarily with group communication dynamics, still others concentrate on organisational communication. A few specialise in platform or public speaking.

Obviously, it is difficult to be a star communicator. For most employees, good communication is mainly devoted to *keeping people well informed*. This means colleagues, superiors, family and friends. Not an easy assignment!

People rated high as communicators are not reluctant to speak up. They can verbalise their feelings. Good communicators do not hide important information from others; they quickly correct misunderstandings through communication, and perhaps most important of all, they *listen*. Good communicators recognise that others need to know enough so that they feel a part of things. Good communicators accept the premise that communication is the life-blood of relationships. In short, if you really want to get along with people, you need to be able to communicate effectively with them.

As a general rule, the following is true:

- Quiet, introspective, introverted people often stay in their shells and undercommunicate. Thus, although they may have a great deal to contribute, they are often misinterpreted.
- Highly verbal, assertive, extroverted people often talk too

much and too forcefully. Thus they run the risk of offending others.

A good communicator is able to keep people informed in a sensitive manner without damaging relationships. Read on and learn why good communicators are also good listeners.

The best communicators are good listeners

As you evaluate yourself as a communicator take into consideration your ability as a listener. Most of us listen at only 25 per cent of our ability. How would your closest friends rate you? Your boss? Your family? Would some people suggest that you should talk less and listen more?

Listed below are some suggestions that can improve your listening skills. Tick those that are applicable to you.

I know how:

☐ To send people signals through my eyes and body gestures so that they know I am listening.

☐ To relax when communicating with others so they will feel comfortable about adding their comments.

☐ To slow my mind down when listening so I won't anticipate what people say before they say it.

☐ To improve my concentration.

☐ To avoid forming a reply before I hear the other person out.

☐ Not to be defensive about my point of view during communication.

☐ To keep my voice soft rather than loud and aggressive.

Case studies

5. Charlie

About three years ago Charlie was deeply hurt and disturbed by something a superior said to him. Since then, communication with that person has been infrequent and emotionally charged. Looking back, Charlie can now see that this lack of communication has damaged his career and made him negative about corporate life in general.

How much of the fault is Charlie's?

6. Melissa

Melissa, known in her hospital ward as the 'quiet nurse', was influenced by her family and Hispanic culture to be submissive and communicate only on special occasions. Although she did well in college and is recognised as a highly skilled registered general nurse, she speaks more to patients than colleagues.

In some respects Melissa is an ideal nurse. She follows the rules, is always on time, never complains and adheres to the suggestions of others even though she does not offer many herself. The only problem is that Melissa is misinterpreted by others because she doesn't communicate. A few think she feels she is too good for her job. Others feel she doesn't like her peers. The supervisor rates her outstanding as an isolated employee but poor as a team member.

If you were Melissa's supervisor, what suggestions would you make in a counselling situation?

Turn to page 94 for the author's views.

Rating yourself as a communicator

So far you have rated yourself on self-esteem and wellness. Now it is time to rate yourself as a communicator. This may be your most difficult evaluation. Take your time and ask yourself the following questions before you circle what you honestly believe is the most accurate number on the scale.

- Do people listen to you?
- Do you receive compliments on your speaking or listening?

- Do you hold back too much when you know you have something important to say?
- Do you initiate conversations?
- Do you feel comfortable when speaking to your supervisor on sensitive subjects?
- Do you consider yourself an expert in communicating over the telephone?
- Do you talk too much?
- Do you speak too loudly? Too softly?

Self-inventory scale
Communications

Low									High
1	2	3	4	5	6	7	8	9	10

CATEGORY 4

How Good Are You at Human Relations?

Staying positive in a negative environment

How positive or negative is your workplace? Do some colleagues have a personality conflict with the boss? Do some employees purposely avoid others? Is there a negative clique of workers who constantly complain and make it more difficult for others?

Some work environments are measurably more positive than others. How positive or negative individual work environments are is often due to the manager in charge. Sometimes morale is due to a combination of factors hard to pinpoint and harder to control. The fact is, the number one reason for job unhappiness and low productivity, centres around relationship conflicts, which in most cases could have been avoided.

Working in a negative environment and keeping yourself positive is not an easy game to play. Yet at one time or another, everyone must deal with the problem. Regardless of your situation, if you are to reach your career goals, your three major human relations challenges are:

- Learning to work with negative people without becoming negative yourself.
- Keeping relationships as healthy as possible – especially with your supervisor.
- Repairing damaged relationships as soon as possible.

The primary reasons why success in these areas will boost your career are:

- Good human relations will improve your personal productivity as well as help others to cooperate to get the job done.
- Your image within the company will be more positive.
- The reduction of personal conflicts will take less out of you and, as a result, make you a more valuable employee.

Tips on how to stay positive

☐ **Tip 1.** Value your own positive attitude to the point where you refuse to let others tarnish it. Keep reminding yourself that your attitude is your most priceless possession, and it belongs to *you* – not your organisation or your family.

☐ **Tip 2.** Be pleasant and communicate with negative colleagues. Encourage them to be more positive by being a good model – but avoid spending too much off-work time (lunch and coffee breaks) with them. Do whatever is necessary to keep your personal productivity up even though those who are negative do not change.

☐ **Tip 3.** Get suggestions from your supervisor on the kind of role he or she wants you to play so that you help to keep departmental morale high. Ask if you are setting a good example. Is it helping? What else can you do? It is good for the supervisor to know you want to contribute to team productivity.

To stay positive when those around you are negative is a difficult challenge, but letting others pull you into their negative way of thinking is a price too high to pay. Those who find the challenge too demanding often move to a new environment and start over again.

Repairing relationships

If good communication is the life-blood of any healthy relationship, then a transfusion of free, open communication should be the first order of business in any relationship repair. It is important to select the right time (when you think the other party will be receptive), the right place (private and free from interruptions), and the discussion should open in a quiet, non-threatening manner.

Once the time and place are 'right' and both parties are comfortable, you should state in your own way that you would like to discuss a win-win system that will restore the relationship and keep it healthy. You should invite the other party to describe what it will take to adjust the system so that both parties will benefit in the future.

It took Jeanne three days to nerve herself to select the right time to open a discussion with Harry over their recent 'falling out'. Although she was awkward in getting the conversation going and introducing her interpretation of a win-win theory, Harry picked up on the idea and within 20 minutes they had constructed a new reward system that formed the basis of a new and better working relationship.

In most one-to-one human situations, some compromise is necessary if the relationship is to be maintained. Often a little 'give' from one end will do the trick. More often, both parties must 'soften' their position from time to time.

Why is compromise often so difficult?

One reason may be because many people establish such rigid and defiant positions to begin with that any compromise could be interpreted as 'weakness' or 'failure'.

Grenville took such a firm stand with his boss about not accepting a temporary assignment that he could not make himself compromise. Later, he discovered his stand had caused a serious conflict and he had second thoughts about compromising but it was too late.

Case study

7. Carole

Despite the fact that Carole knows she cannot easily duplicate her salary or benefits with a competitor, she has decided to give her supervisor two weeks' notice this Friday. Her decision is based upon protecting her mental health. The working climate she must endure has become so negative she is in a continual state of depression.

Carole knows that the company has provided good physical working conditions. No complaint there! It is simply the negative attitudes of three colleagues that are part of her team. These three individuals (all senior to Carole) are so bitter about life that she becomes irritated and negative herself. Even the efforts of the supervisor, who is aware of the problem, have been to no avail.

Is Carole making a good decision?

To compare your answer with that of the author, turn to page 94.

Appraising your human relations skills

As we have seen, some people are measurably better at protecting themselves from the negative attitudes of others. These lucky individuals seem able to throw up a protective shield and stay positive no matter what. These same people are often good at creating positive relationships and repairing them when things turn sour. We can call these workers *human relations smart!*

How good are you at protecting your positive attitude and working well with others? As you rate yourself on the scale below, take the following into consideration:

- The value you place on your positive attitude
- The importance you attach to good human relations
- Your tolerance level regarding the behaviour of others
- Your freedom from prejudice

- Your sensitivity to the relationship between good human relations and productivity.

If you have the reputation among your colleagues of being excellent at human relations, it is in order for you to circle an 8, 9, or in a rare case, 10. If you are frequently negative and it hurts your personal as well as group productivity, give yourself 5 or under.

Self-inventory scale
Staying positive and working well with others

Low									High
1	2	3	4	5	6	7	8	9	10

CATEGORY 5
Are You Taking Yourself Too Seriously?

Developing a sense of humour

Some individuals have the capacity to take a serious situation and 'flip it over' so they can find a humorous perspective that may lie underneath. When they find something that is laughable and then share it with others, everyone makes a better adjustment. In the world of work, such people are invaluable.

Humour, deep down inside, is an expression of joy that comes from being free. It is a form of communication. It is fun to laugh. According to many medical experts, laughter is a therapeutic experience. But humour does not come as easily to some as it does to others. Thus, to develop a sense of humour requires an awareness of its value to the person who makes the effort. Ask yourself these questions:

- Do you view humour as a way to enhance your career?
- Do you regard telling laughable stories or jokes as a way of building better relationships with others?
- Do you feel that many people take life too seriously? Including yourself?
- What is your humour quotient? That is, just how good are you at dispensing humour?

To find an answer to the last question, please turn the page and continue.

Exercise: Humour quotient

Read the statements and circle the number where you feel you belong. If you circle a 7, you are saying the statement is 'very characteristic of you'; if you circle a 1, the statement is 'very uncharacteristic of you'. Be honest – no one is watching!

1. My boss would describe me as a 'Humour Asset' because my sense of humour benefits the company.   7 6 5 4 3 2 1

2. My colleagues and family would list my sense of humour as one of my greatest assets.   7 6 5 4 3 2 1

3. I avoid sarcasm, ethnic and negative humour except in private conversations with close friends.   7 6 5 4 3 2 1

4. I can laugh at my own mistakes and enjoy occasionally being poked fun at.   7 6 5 4 3 2 1

5. I laugh alone when I feel something is funny.   7 6 5 4 3 2 1

6. As a humour consumer, I laugh easily and enjoy laughing at jokes and stories others share.   7 6 5 4 3 2 1

7. I seek out cartoons, comedy shows, comedians and other humour stimulants.   7 6 5 4 3 2 1

8. I write down humorous stories and keep cartoons and articles that promote humour.   7 6 5 4 3 2 1

9. When stressed on the job, my sense of humour helps me to keep my perspective.   7 6 5 4 3 2 1

10. I spontaneously look for the funny side of life and share it with others.   7 6 5 4 3 2 1

11. I send humorous notes and cartoons to friends, colleagues and customers.   7 6 5 4 3 2 1

12. My sense of humour makes it hard for people to be cross with me.   7 6 5 4 3 2 1

13. I love to tell humorous stories to make my point in on-the-job communication.   7 6 5 4 3 2 1

14. I sometimes act silly at unexpected times.   7 6 5 4 3 2 1

15. I am not uncomfortable laughing out loud with colleagues.   7 6 5 4 3 2 1

16. I use humour to help myself and others recall important things.   7 6 5 4 3 2 1

If you score 100–112 you are lying or can't add up; a score between 90 and 99, indicates 'Humour Pro'; a score of 70–89 means minor adjustments may be in order; a score of 45–69 suggests a major adjustment is needed; a score below 45 may require a 'humour transplant'. If you did not laugh or smile at this scoring, give yourself a zero!

Fun in the workplace

Holding down a job is serious business. Building a career within the structure of a corporation is a demanding adventure. Productivity levels are important. To stay in the job they must be maintained, and to advance they should be increased. Skills must be honed. Quality must be achieved. Work is work!

But all work, now and then, needs an injection of lightness for the following reasons:

- Employees can get so serious and tense that appropriate humour can increase productivity, not diminish it.
- Laughter among a working 'team' will increase the spirit and motivation of all members.
- The right amount of humour can help to create and maintain positive working relationships that benefit everyone.

A sense of humour is also necessary in building a successful career. That is why it has been included as one of the 12 most important work qualities in the inventory (profile) on page 74.

You have probably known someone who is highly capable mentally, well educated, and seems to have *everything* – but never reaches her or his potential. The reason? Often it is because of the missing ingredient – a sense of humour.

Whatever your career goal may be, you are encouraged to be a professional. But a professional without a sense of humour may not reach his or her goal – and will not have nearly as much fun getting there!

Case study

8. Trudy

Yesterday was a big event for Trudy because she was invited to be the manager of her department. The invitation was given when she and her manager were asked to meet the director of her division and the director of human resources. The divisional director announced that she was the company choice for the promotion. Then the director of human resources talked about her new salary and when she would attend her first management training seminar. Trudy was excited; it was a big day!

When the meeting ended, Trudy thanked everyone and asked if a question would be in order. The group agreed, so she asked: 'I'm curious to know why I was selected in preference to others with more training and experience.' Everyone looked to her supervisor for an answer. He replied: 'It was your positive sense of humour.'

Do you agree or disagree that a sense of humour is important enough to make the difference in selecting one candidate rather than another?

Turn to page 95 and compare your answer with that of the author.

Rating yourself on humour

Your humour quotient (page 34) indicates your ability to use humour. It does not necessarily measure how often you use humour, how successful you are at it, or what impact humour has on your attitude and job productivity. In completing the scale below, analyse how you use humour in your workplace.

- Do you use as *much* humour as you should?
- Does your use of humour keep you from taking your job too seriously?
- Do you weave some form of humour into most of your conversations?
- Do you constantly *look* for humour in problem or negative situations?
- Do you contribute significantly to team spirit through your sense of humour?

If you rate yourself 8 or above, you are saying you make better use of humour than others in your work environment. If you rate yourself from 4 to 7, you are saying that you contribute your share. A rating of 3 or less is a signal that your humour quotient needs work.

Self-inventory scale *Sense of humour*									
Low									High
1	2	3	4	5	6	7	8	9	10

CATEGORY 6
Does Your Attitude Need a Positive Boost?

The need for frequent attitude renewal

Everyone – employees, students, homemakers, retirees – must occasionally engage in some form of attitude renewal or adjustment. There is no escape.

Renewal means to restore or refresh your view; rejuvenate your approach; re-establish your positive focus; and/or repair the damage of wear and tear to your attitude.

Weekends, holidays and time off are frequently used as 'pit stops' for attitude adjustment purposes. They are necessary to combat the following:

1. External shock waves

As a seismograph records the intensity and duration of an earthquake, your attitude reflects tremors caused by financial reversals, personal disappointments, family problems, health concerns, and so on. There is no way to insulate yourself fully from these shock waves.

2. Self-image problems

We frequently become critical of the way we appear to ourselves. Maybe we have put on a few pounds or are not as well groomed as we were in the past. This creates a negative self-image – a kind of dirty lens that keeps us from thinking of ourselves in a positive way. When this happens, working on a better image is mandatory. Health clubs, clothing shops, fashion boutiques, hairdressers and beauty parlours are, in effect, attitude adjustment stations.

3. Negative drift

Nobody can explain why it happens, but sometimes, even when the environment is calm and you have a good self-image, there can be a movement towards a negative attitude. Some blame this drift on the negative aspects in today's society. The feeling is that because you are bombarded with so many negative stimuli through news stories, you tend to become more negative by osmosis.

Regardless of the reason – environmental shock waves, self-image problems or negative drift – everyone needs to adjust his or her attitude on occasion.

Attitude renewal at the first level is a daily process. For some, a few moments of meditation may be the answer. Others, who seem to get off to a bad start, have learned to phone a friend mid-morning for a 'boost'. Still others use music or comedy as part of their daily routine.

What is a positive attitude?

On the surface, attitude is the way you communicate your mood to others. When you are optimistic and anticipate successful encounters, you transmit a positive attitude and people usually respond favourably. When you are pessimistic and expect the worst, your attitude is often negative and people tend to avoid you. Inside your head, where it all starts, attitude is a mind set. *It is the way you look at things mentally.*

Think of attitude as your mental focus on the outside world. Like using a camera, you can focus or set your mind on what appeals to you. You can see situations as either opportunities or failures: a cold winter day as either beautiful or ugly, a departmental meeting as interesting or boring. Perception – the complicated process of viewing and interpreting your environment – is a mental phenomenon. It is within your power to concentrate on selected aspects of your environment and ignore others. Quite simply, you take the picture of life you want to take.

Emphasising the positive and diffusing the negative is like using a magnifying glass. You can place the glass over good news and feel better, or you can magnify bad news and make yourself miserable. Magnifying situations can become a habit. If you continually focus on difficult situations, the result will be exaggerated distortion of problems. A better approach might be to imagine you have binoculars. Use the magnifying end to view positive things, and reverse them (using the other end) whenever you encounter negative elements, to make them appear smaller. Once you are able to alter your imagery to highlight the positive, you are on the right road.

The challenge of staying positive

Attitude is never static. It is a continual, dynamic, sensitive, perceptual process. Unless you are on constant guard, negative factors can slip into your perspective. This will cause you to spend 'mind time' on difficulties rather than opportunities.

If negative factors stay around long enough, they will be reflected in your disposition. The positive is still there, but it has been overshadowed by the negative.

It is a challenge to push the negative factors to the outer perimeter of your thinking. Those who learn this trick will reflect it, and others will notice.

Of course, no one can be positive all the time. Excessive optimism – like Pollyanna's in the novels by Eleanor Porter – is not realistic. Friends and business associates will probably feel it is artificial. After all, a positive attitude is not an act; it must be genuine. Sometimes, when things get really difficult, a positive attitude may be impossible or even inappropriate. The 'we shall overcome' perspective is more determination based upon rightful indignation than that of a positive attitude.

When things are going well, a positive attitude becomes self-reinforcing and easy to maintain. Being human, however, ensures that something will always happen to test your positive mind set. Some person or situation is always on the horizon to step on your attitude and challenge your ability to bounce back.

You keep your positive attitude when you give it away

When you are frustrated by the behaviour of others, you may be tempted to give them 'a piece of your mind'. This is understandable. It is a better policy, however, to give them 'a piece of your positive attitude'. When you do this, it allows others to adjust your attitude for you.

> Sharon asked Carolyn to meet her for lunch because she needed a psychological lift. Carolyn didn't feel like it, but she accepted and made a special effort to be positive. When the luncheon was over, Carolyn had not only given Sharon a boost, she felt better herself. Both parties benefited.

When you give a part of your positive attitude to others, you create a symbiotic relationship. The recipient feels better, but so do you. It is interesting but true that *you keep your positive attitude by giving it away*.

When it comes to giving your positive attitude to others, you can be generous and selfish at the same time.

> Mrs Lindsey is considered a master teacher. The primary reason is that she freely shares her positive attitude with students and colleagues. In return, students and fellow teachers are constantly reinforcing Mrs Lindsey's attitude with compliments and attention.
>
> Mr Trent is an outstanding office manager. He is also a tease. Every day he creates a little levity to balance the pressure of work. In sharing his good humour he is rewarded by a dedicated staff that work hard to deliver higher productivity because they appreciate the pleasant work environment.

Case study

9. Shirley

At Shirley's last performance review her supervisor gave her a 'fair' rating on attitude instead of good or excellent. Shirley thought she deserved better and challenged the rating. During the discussion that followed, her supervisor said she felt Shirley could be more friendly with clients, patient with colleagues, positive on the telephone, and also be more communicative.

The rating was not changed and, as a result, Shirley almost resigned. But after talking it over with her husband, she decided that maybe her supervisor was sending her a message, so she decided to change her focus and concentrate on being more positive. Three months later her husband said: 'Shirley, I have noticed a big improvement in our relationship. You are more fun than in the past and all our friends are talking about it.'

Is it possible for an attitude change in one environment (work) to improve one's focus in another environment (social)?

Compare your view with that of the author on page 95.

Assessing your attitude

Assessing someone else's attitude is a sensitive and dangerous undertaking, as Shirley's supervisor discovered. It is also difficult to assess your own attitude. We all have a tendency to feel we are more positive than other people may interpret us as being.

Before completing the 1 to 10 scale below, ask yourself:

- Do you see yourself as a highly positive person with only occasional down periods?
- Over the long haul, are you measurably more positive than other colleagues?
- Do you consider your positive attitude to be your most priceless possession?

- Do colleagues sometimes ask you: 'How do you manage to stay so positive?'

If you gave yourself 'yes' answers to the above questions, do not hesitate to circle 8, 9 or possibly 10. If you sense you can be measurably more positive in the future, circle a lower number.

Self-inventory scale
Attitude

Low									High
1	2	3	4	5	6	7	8	9	10

CATEGORY 7
Are You Sufficiently Assertive?

How to develop positive assertiveness

It would be nice if you could simply decide to go down the road marked 'Assertive' and live your life without straying from the path.

Real life is full of twists and turns and *no one is consistently assertive*. We all use the three basic behaviour styles described below depending on the situation and personal factors. The good news is that *we can learn to become more assertive more of the time*.

1. **Non-assertive behaviour** is passive and indirect. It communicates a message of inferiority. By being non-assertive we allow the wants, needs and rights of others to be more important than our own. Non-assertive behaviour helps to create win-lose situations. A person behaving non-assertively will lose (or at best be disregarded) while allowing others to win. Following this road leads to being a victim, not a winner.

2. **Aggressive behaviour** is more complex. It can be either active or passive. Aggression can be direct or indirect, honest or dishonest, but it always communicates an impression of superiority and disrespect. By being aggressive we put our wants, needs and rights above those of others. We attempt to get our way by not allowing others a choice. Aggressive behaviour is usually inappropriate because it violates the rights of others. People behaving aggressively may 'win' by making sure others

'lose' – but in doing so set themselves up for retaliation. No one likes a bully.

3. Assertive behaviour is active, direct and honest. It communicates an impression of self-respect and respect for others. By being assertive we view our wants, needs and rights as equal with those of others. We work towards win-win outcomes. An assertive person 'wins' by influencing, listening and negotiating so that others choose to cooperate willingly. This behaviour leads to success without retaliation and encourages honest, open relationships!

Exercise: An assertiveness quiz

Before learning how to develop your assertiveness, it is important to take a few moments to get some idea of where you are right now. Answer the questions below honestly. They will help you to gain some insights into your current level of assertiveness.

Assign a number to each item using this scale:

Always				Never
5	4	3	2	1

_____ 1. I ask others to do things without feeling guilty or anxious.

_____ 2. When someone asks me to do something I don't want to do, I say 'No' without feeling guilty or anxious.

_____ 3. I am comfortable when speaking to a large group of people.

_____ 4. I confidently express my honest opinions to authority figures (such as my boss).

_____ 5. When I experience powerful feelings (anger, frustration, disappointment, etc), I express them easily.

_____ 6. When I express anger, I do so without blaming others for 'making me furious'.

_____ 7. I am comfortable speaking up in a group situation.

_____ 8. If I disagree with the majority opinion in a meeting, I can 'stick to my guns' without feeling uncomfortable or being abrasive.

_____ 9. When I make a mistake, I will acknowledge it.

_____ 10. I tell others when their behaviour creates a problem for me.

_____ 11. Meeting new people in social situations is something I do with ease and comfort.

_____ 12. When discussing my beliefs, I do so without labelling the opinions of others as 'crazy', 'stupid', 'ridiculous', or 'irrational'.

_____ 13. I assume that most people are competent and trustworthy and do not have difficulty delegating tasks to others.

_____ 14. When considering doing something for the first time, I feel confident I can learn to do it.

_____ 15. I believe my needs are as important as those of others and I am entitled to have my needs satisfied.

TOTAL SCORE (sum of the 15 numbers)

If your total is 60 or higher, you have a consistently assertive philosophy and probably handle most situations well. If your total is 45–60 you have a fairly assertive outlook. If your total is 30–44, your natural response is often non-assertive or aggressive. If your total is 15–29 you have considerable difficulty being assertive.

Case studies

10. Kim

Assume your name is Alice, and Kim Aoki, who was raised and educated in Japan, has become one of your best friends. You work closely together in company headquarters. Kim is excellent in computer programming, dealing with accounting systems, and her English is impeccable. But she is having trouble adjusting to British culture.

Kim is quiet, unassuming, and quickly moves to the background when her position is challenged by others. Last night the two of you were discussing the problem in an open but probing way. When you ask Kim why she finds it so difficult to stand up for herself, she replies: 'It is the way I was brought up. I feel uncomfortable when there are confrontations of any kind.' You reply: 'How can I help you?' Kim says: 'I just want to be more assertive, more like you.'

How would you go about helping Kim?

11. Joanne
Joanne is outstanding when it comes to setting up office procedures that take advantage of available computer technology. As a result, she is successful despite her abrasive way in working with people. Management puts up with Joanne because she gets the job done, but closer observation would signal that she leaves a wake of unhappy and less productive employees behind. As one colleague put it: 'Joanne took an assertiveness seminar and she turned out to be aggressive. She has great potential but few people want to be near her.'

If you were Joanne's supervisor, how would you go about reversing the process so that she would turn her overbearing manner into a natural and pleasant assertiveness?

Turn to page 95 for author's comments on both cases.

Assertiveness self-assessment scale

It may be more difficult to rate yourself on assertiveness than any of the other 11 factors involved in the profile. Why? Because you circle the highest number only if you feel you have the exact balance between aggressiveness and non-assertiveness. For example, if you frequently demonstrate aggressive behaviour (such as becoming emotionally involved to the point that you talk too much, push people around, or generally disregard the needs of others), you should not circle any number higher than a 5. On the other hand, if you are so non-assertive that you are often ignored while others are consulted, here again you should not circle any number higher than a 5.

However, if you sincerely believe you are not non-assertive and not aggressive, you can rate yourself somewhere above 5.

- If you feel you have just the right degree of assertiveness, give yourself 9 or 10.
- If you are pleased with your assertiveness but know there is some room for improvement, circle number 7 or 8.
- If you are not pleased with your progress towards the degree of assertiveness you believe to be right for you, circle 6 or lower.

Self-inventory scale
Assertiveness

Low									High
1	2	3	4	5	6	7	8	9	10

CATEGORY 8
Do Your Job Skills Need to be Upgraded?

The winds of change

Not only do organisations change (restructuring) but the jobs within them also have new dimensions. This is especially true when the positions are technical by nature and must, therefore, improve when new technology arrives. Job descriptions these days seldom remain static for more than a few months.

What does this mean to the individual who occupies the position? It means that those who wish to be successful must stay flexible and open to new experiences.

- It may mean additional training, either on the job or in a special class.
- It may mean attending a company-sponsored seminar.
- It may mean engaging in a self-help programme with the assistance of a manual or new machine.

All jobs have certain skills that need to be upgraded frequently. New equipment, supplies, procedures or techniques all need to be mastered as soon as possible. It is difficult to find a job where additional training is not required or desirable.

What does it all mean? It means that skill or competence upgrading is a constant responsibility of the worker. Those who accept the challenge prepare themselves for advancement; those who reject the challenge find themselves shuffled into less demanding jobs. As long as the winds of change are blowing, re-training, skill upgrading and new approaches to excellence will be in vogue.

It is necessary for organisational survival.

Exercise: Measuring the degree of change in your job

Some jobs change faster than others. For example, those connected with the computer or communication industries must change quickly to keep up with the new technology; jobs in some service occupations (selling, food preparation, delivery) usually change at a slower pace, but change none the less.

What about the job you currently occupy? To discover the speed at which it is changing, answer the following questions.

		Yes	No
1.	Have you operated any new equipment in the past year?	____	____
2.	Have some colleagues passed you as far as selected skills are concerned?	____	____
3.	Do you find yourself asking others to bring you up to date on new procedures or techniques?	____	____
4.	Has your attitude towards change become more negative in recent months?	____	____
5.	Are you avoiding methods to upgrade your skills even when you know it would be wise for you to do so?	____	____
6.	Are you uncomfortable with the number of mistakes you are making?	____	____
7.	Have you given up trying for a promotion because you realise your skills are no longer up to par?	____	____

8. Has there been a decrease in your productivity because of changes in your job specification? _____ _____

9. Do you sense you are falling behind others in the skill/competence race? _____ _____

10. Has your superior suggested either that you sign up for a company-sponsored seminar or return to school for upgrading purposes? _____ _____

If you gave seven or more Yes answers, it would appear that you should make immediate arrangements to profit from some additional training. If you gave five, six or seven Yes answers, the need is less urgent. If you gave four or fewer Yes answers, you appear to be keeping up with the competence requirements of your profession.

Case study

12. Felicity

Felicity is sick and tired of having to improve her computer skills all the time. She no sooner becomes comfortable with one machine or piece of software than something new comes along. All she wants, really, is a job that is not over-demanding so she can save her mental and physical energy for her family and personal life.

Yesterday, to her surprise, Felicity was offered an opportunity to become a supervisor in her department. Ah, she thought, this is for me. I can keep good relationships with everyone but I can delegate all the skill stuff to others who like it more than I do. I will also have more freedom.

Is Felicity making a logical decision?

To match your thoughts with those of the author turn to page 96.

Skill level scale

You are now invited to rate yourself on how well you have mastered the skills that are required in your present job. Such skills or competencies might include the quality of your written communications, skills connected with a computer, mechanical skills, financial or accounting skills, etc. A job description usually includes these or other specific skills required for top performance in a job.

In rating yourself, keep in mind that you are comparing your skill level (speed, accuracy, depth, etc) with others in similar jobs *only*. Also include the skill with which you deal with customers, either in person or on the telephone. Few people reach a 10 level, but a score of 1, 2 or 3 may mean you are on probation until your skill level is increased.

Self-inventory scale
Skill-level

Low									High
1	2	3	4	5	6	7	8	9	10

CATEGORY 9
Are You Satisfied With the Quality of Your Work?

The switch to excellence

There has been a noticeable movement in the direction of higher quality products and improved service in the past few years. The pursuit of excellence is a reality. There are four major reasons for this trend.

- Product safety has been highlighted by consumer pressure groups and legal implications have followed.
- Organisations have become more aware of their environmental and social responsibilities.
- Repeat sales depend more upon customer satisfaction (quality) than in the past.
- International competition has set higher quality standards for some products.

All this has caused higher management to place a greater emphasis on quality. Trains are expected to run on time; airlines are expected to compensate overbooked passengers who are left behind; local education authorities are expected to meet the needs of children in their areas; hospitals are expected to carry out operations on patients in pain or distress without undue delay.

Sacrificing quality for speed or total output has always been a questionable policy. Now, almost everyone accepts the belief that it is better to stay as close as possible to zero defect quality standards before concentrating on speed or output. This quality first, speed second philosophy has been shown to improve the profit picture of the organisation. Especially in the long run.

Exercise: Quality questionnaire

This exercise is designed to measure your attitude towards quality work as opposed to average standards. *Quality is a frame of mind.* Some organisations are more successful in getting high quality work from their employees than others.

Please tick Yes or No for each statement.

	Yes	No
1. I would take personal pride in working for a firm that demands quality standards.	____	____
2. I feel good about doing something right even if it is routine work, and I must perform the same function over and over again.	____	____
3. I like being orderly, organised and efficient. It bothers me to make a mistake.	____	____
4. I would prefer to be reprimanded for being slow rather than sloppy.	____	____
5. I have little patience with anyone who has a 'get by' attitude.	____	____
6. Speed is to be admired in any job as long as quality is not sacrificed.	____	____
7. I would rather re-do a lengthy report in my own time than submit it with a single error.	____	____
8. You can't call yourself a professional in any job unless you put quality first.	____	____

9. I believe in the two phrases 'haste makes waste' and 'safety first'. _____ _____

10. I enjoy doing things right even if no one will know about it but me. _____ _____

The more Yes answers you gave yourself the more positive your attitude is towards quality work. Five No answers may be a signal that the quality of your efforts could show improvement.

Case study

13. Victor

Victor has the mental capacity to move in many directions at the same time and still do a better than average job on most projects. But occasionally he moves so fast that, along the way, quality suffers. You are Victor's superior and you would like to prepare him to be your replacement. He has outstanding leadership ability. The only major characteristic that bothers you is his willingness to sacrifice a small degree of excellence.

You devise three separate strategies which you feel might convince Victor that quality will make him more valuable to the company – and also more promotable. Your strategies are:

1. Construct an imaginary case that demonstrates how quality took a person into a top management circle ahead of others. Discuss it with Victor.

2. Explain why your boss is such an advocate of excellence through a discussion of the firm's expressed mission – *'Excellence above all'*.

3. Tell a story about yourself where you made a serious mistake by not putting quality ahead of everything else.

Which strategy would you employ to convince Victor? Why?

Compare with the author's response on page 96.

Quality work performance scale

Now that you have expressed yourself regarding quality work standards, rate yourself on the quality aspects of your current performance in the job *you hold now*. As you do this on the scale below, please keep the following in mind:

- A 10 rating means quality perfection which may be impossible to achieve in most jobs.
- A 1 rating means you have no concern for quality. 'Getting by' without getting caught is your goal.
- A 5 rating means you are average in quality work performance for *your kind of job in your firm*.

Be as honest and objective as possible. Circle the number that reflects your actual performance, not what you hope it will be in the future.

Self-inventory scale
Quality work performance

Low									High
1	2	3	4	5	6	7	8	9	10

CATEGORY 10
Do You Have Your Career and Lifestyle Organised?

Self-management is the key

According to Paul M Timm, author of *Successful Self-Management*, an acceptable definition of self-management would be:

> The *process* of maximising our *time and talents* to achieve *worthwhile goals* while achieving a *balanced life*.

Note the key words:

Process. Self-management is continuous. It is not something we do only once or occasionally. We make it a process by adopting some simple 'rituals' or 'routines' into our daily lives.

Time and talents. These are unique personal resources that we alone can manage. In essence, it is *through* our time and talent that we manage people, finances, etc.

Worthwhile goals. These are the outcomes of our efforts – our planned achievements. Our rewards! To be truly worthwhile, such goals must be rooted in a sound value system.

Balanced life. A primary challenge is managing our careers in such a way that we have time to manage our personal lifestyles and leisure time. In other words, organised people find greater fulfilment in their personal lives.

To summarise, self-management is more than just making the best use of our time. It is making maximum use of our talents by setting daily, weekly, monthly and longer-term goals and proceeding to reach them through various self-management techniques.

The nuts and bolts of time and task management

Most time management experts agree that rule number one in a thoughtful planning process is some form of notebook, diary or planner in which you can write things down.

How much time should you devote to daily planning? It will vary with each individual, but a minimum of 10 or 15 minutes a day solely devoted to planning is recommended. Use the steps described below and you should see a significant increase in your personal effectiveness.*

How to do effective daily task planning

1. Develop a priority task list for each day
Prioritising tasks helps us to sort them out, decide which need to be attacked first, and which can be saved for later.

2. Assign a letter priority to each item on your list
Use **A**, **B**, **C** or ★ (star) and put the letter **A** next to items that *must* be done. These are critical to you. You alone determine whether they are critical or not. This decision is based on your values and goals. Tasks required either by outside forces (like your boss) or internal ones (such as a personal commitment) will normally receive an **A** priority.

Use the letter **B** to indicate *should do* items. These are things that should be done, items that are really worth spending time on. They aren't quite as critical as the **A**s, but they're nevertheless important.

The letter **C** is for *could do* items. These are things worth listing,

---

* These steps were adapted from *Successful Self-Management* by Paul R Timm (Kogan Page).

and worth thinking about. And if you get the **A**s and **B**s completed, worth doing.

A star ★ indicates an item that is *urgent* – something that *must* be done *now*! it is both important and vital. You've got to get on it right away. These items occasionally come up during a working day (ie, a crisis). When you add them to your list, put a star by them, and drop whatever else you're doing, even if it's an **A** item – and complete that task.

3. *Assign a number to your tasks*
You can further sharpen your plan of attack by assigning a number to each task.

Use the numbering system as a chronological indicator. That is, ask which task should you realistically do first. If you have a meeting at two in the afternoon and it's an **A** item, it may not be **A-1**, simply because there are other things to do earlier in the day. As with other priorities, you decide how to best use it, but a number system will provide your marching orders.

Case studies

14. Rita and Ralph
Rita leaves her job each afternoon without a plan for the following day. Her strategy is to shed work responsibilities quickly so she can pursue her personal lifestyle. In defence of her pattern, Rita claims she is so exhausted by the end of the day that planning ahead would be ineffective. However, as soon as she is in the middle of her 40-minute journey the next morning, she thinks about her plans for the day. She often uses a notebook to organise her thoughts.

Ralph is always the last to leave work, usually 30 minutes after his last employee has left. A highly organised person, he finishes many details and then quietly sets down his priorities for the following day in his desk diary. Ralph claims this helps him to leave all work problems behind so he can enjoy his lifestyle to the fullest. He doesn't think about business until he shows up at his desk the following morning.

Which plan would work best for you? Is your present plan superior?

_____

_____

_____

See author's preference on page 96.

15. Daisy

Daisy, a single parent, is most efficient and is respected as an office manager. Over the years, she has learned and applied the techniques of self-management to her career with outstanding results. With her time-planning notebook to hand, she makes maximum use of her time and achieves high standards from her employees.

Things are very different in her personal life. For some reason, she refuses to apply her self-management techniques at home. Result? Her home is such a mess she refuses to invite friends to call in. Her car is always breaking down, owing to lack of maintenance. And without an organised wardrobe her appearance often leaves much to be desired. Worst of all, she does not follow a diet and is seriously overweight.

When a close friend, Shelley, recently suggested to Daisy that she was making a mistake by not applying her self-management techniques to her lifestyle, she replied: 'Shell, down deep inside I hate being an organised person. Somehow, it causes me to tighten up and lose my sense of joy and creativity. I force myself to be organised in my career because I couldn't hold a management job without it, but when the working day is over I need the relaxation that comes from being disorganised. For me, it is a kind of balance to keep my sanity.'

Do you agree with Daisy? If you were Shelley, what argument

would you advance to convince her she should apply her self-management techniques at home?

_____

_____

_____

Turn to page 96 to compare your thoughts with those of the author.

Self-management evaluation

Some people manage themselves in a quiet, efficient, systematic and consistent manner. In so doing, they accomplish their professional and personal goals. These individuals take great pride in being organised and they enjoy the process. They should rate themselves an 8 or higher.

Other people seem to manage themselves rather well but do it reluctantly and inconsistently. They force the process and do not enjoy it. They should rate themselves somewhere between 4 and 7.

Still others let other people and their environment manage _them_. Circumstances dictate their behaviour. Their job activities and personal lives are chaotic. The results usually spell career stagnation or worse. These individuals should rate themselves 4 or under.

Self-inventory scale _Self-management_									
Low									**High**
1	2	3	4	5	6	7	8	9	10

CATEGORY 11
Are You Reaching Your Creativity Potential?

Everyone has a creativity potential

It may come as a surprise to you that creativity is included as one of the 12 self-improvement categories. Many people, unfortunately, feel that creativity is confined to those with above average artistic talent or the ability to think on a conceptual level. Not so. Everyone has the potential to be creative in their own way.

Creativity in the work environment is any thought that manifests itself into a suggestion that will increase productivity. Simple ideas often are the best. Doing something only slightly differently can produce a saving in the use of paper, improve employee morale, or increase efficiency through the rearranging of office furniture. Of course, creativity can also include more complex ideas that improve the quality of products and service to customers, and at the same time solve major problems. The point is that creativity is not limited to selected individuals or blockbuster ideas.

It is easy to recognise the desirability for creativity in an advertising agency. Yet creativity can be equally important in a shipping department or office job.

You might conclude that your job is uncreative because it involves mostly routine tasks. If so, take a second look. You may be passing up excellent opportunities to contribute some imaginative ideas and along the way improve your possibilities of career advancement.

In the past, some organisations have encouraged suggestions from employees by offering prizes or placing suggestion boxes around the building. A better approach might be to distribute 'creativity envelopes' along with pay packets so ideas could be submitted to obtain special rewards and recognition. All suggestions spring from creative roots!

Case study

16. Jerry

At college, Jerry was always referred to as the 'ideas man' by his friends. Some of Jerry's ideas were really over the top. Others were down to earth and practical. Everyone reckoned he would wind up making films or doing some kind of highly creative work.

In Jerry's first job with a large marketing firm, he took three months to get the lie of the land. Then, almost every week, he would submit a marketing idea – one connected with packaging, buying incentives or how to improve sales via the various media. All his ideas were submitted verbally to his supervisor, Sally North. After more than two months and not having heard anything about his ideas, he confronted Ms North. Her reply was: 'The first time I get an idea from you that shows maturity, you will have my support.'

Two months and about six good ideas without a response later, Jerry decided on a new strategy. Instead of submitting his ideas verbally, he would present them in a creative manner (special artwork, etc) to both Ms North and her superior. In Jerry's mind, this in itself would show creativity as well as bring attention to his ideas.

What is your opinion of Jerry's strategy?

_____

_____

_____

_____

See page 97 for the author's comments.

Creativity assessment

Your challenge on this page is to do your best in evaluating your creative contributions during the past year. Ask yourself these questions:

- Have you been underestimating your creative nature and, as a result, making fewer creative contributions than would otherwise be the case?
- Is your failure to make more creative suggestions slowing your career progress?
- Have you had ideas at work that you feel would improve productivity but failed to submit them?
- Has your mind produced some creative ideas that you kept to yourself?
- Would a 'second look' at your present job show more creative opportunities than you have seen in the past?

If you have been going along without using your creative powers, rate yourself a 5 or under. If, however, you have been using your creativity to improve your job or the productivity of your department, rate yourself higher. If you have been improving your present job, helping to develop a better department, and on top of that, submitting creative ideas to improve your company as a whole, give yourself a 9 or a 10.

Self-inventory scale *Creativity*									
Low									**High**
1	2	3	4	5	6	7	8	9	10

CATEGORY 12
Can You Stop Procrastinating?

Are you a procrastinator?

Millions of people, with otherwise good intentions, postpone important things they know they should be doing. You're one of them if you respond positively to each of the following statements. (Be truthful.)

1. I know who and what I am . . . but I want something better!

2. I'm frustrated because I can't do everything I want to.

3. I'm delaying an important task I know I should be working on and that bothers me. (Your task could be: asking for a rise, finishing a report, calling on a prospect, starting a new career, studying for an examination, etc.) Add your own:

   My task: _____

4. My task is important because this is what will happen if I don't do it:

   The consequence: _____

   _____

5. My task has a beginning, an ending, and a definite outcome (eg making a sale, getting a rise, producing a document).

   The beginning: _____

   The ending: _____

The specific outcome: _____

6. There is a specific day, month, hour or year on which I hope to have my task completed and I know what's early and what's late.

    The completion date: _____

7. I am deliberately doing something else to avoid my task (eg eating, drinking, sleeping, playing dead, playing tennis, being busy). Add your own:

    My delaying tactics: _____

8. I know in my heart that I really should be doing this task and I feel guilty about not doing it.

    Yes _____ No _____

Exercise: Major causes of procrastination

The causes that follow aren't listed in any particular order of magnitude or importance. Tick those that cause you to procrastinate.

☐ Confusion

☐ Lack of priorities

☐ Lack of responsibility

☐ Fear of risk-taking

☐ Escape from unpleasant tasks

☐ Anxiety or depression

☐ Obsessive/Compulsive behaviour

☐ Monotony or boredom

☐ Fatigue

☐ Outside distractions

☐ Lack of analytical ability

- [ ] Forgetfulness
- [ ] Dependence on others
- [ ] Manipulation of others
- [ ] Physical disabilities

Add your own:

- [ ] _____
- [ ] _____

How to stop procrastinating for good

Are you angry and frustrated? Do you regularly have delays and postponements that keep you from reaching your goals and objectives? If so, here's a simple, straightforward procedure that will help you to break the procrastination habit and start you moving on the road to success.

Take these four steps and put an end to procrastination once and for all:

1. Acknowledge the simple fact that you procrastinate. Then make up your mind to stop doing it.

    I have procrastinated in the past, but I'm not going to do it any more.

    Signed: _____

    Date: _____

2. Learn as much as you can about procrastination.

    - Recognise what it is.
    - Work out why you do it.
    - Find out what you can do to stop.

3. Make a list of specific things you're going to start doing right away to break this bad habit.

First, I'm going to: _____

Then, I'll: _____

Finally, I'll: _____

4. Carry out your plan of action.

Commit yourself to getting rid of procrastination and do it now!

Case study

17. John

John is forever taking seminars and reading self-help books in an effort to improve himself. Once finished, he vows he will improve in that area. The only problem is that within a few days, he is back into his old pattern and no permanent behavioural changes have been accomplished.

As his supervisor, you decide to give John a system that will help him to change his behaviour so he can take advantage of what he learns. The system is a simple one. It recommends that, having completed a seminar or self-help book, John write down between five and seven changes he would like to make: never fewer than five or more than seven. Then, after three days, you go over his list with him, asking which changes are most important. After selecting the one that John is convinced will do the most for him, have him write a big red tick next to it.

You instruct John to make the ticked change an all-important objective for an entire week. Concentrate on it. Talk about it. Change habits to accommodate it.

Then, once John feels he has made the change permanent, he can go back to his original list and select another change or wait until another idea comes from a different source. Your motto is: One important change at a time!

Will the change system work for John?

See page 97 for the author's comments.

Don't postpone this rating

You have now appraised your personal and career status in 11 significant areas. It is time for you to rate yourself on *how much initiative you normally demonstrate*. Obviously, if you are known as a procrastinator you deserve a low rating (5 or under) on this scale. But if you are not a procrastinator, how should you rate yourself?

- If you feel you could *modestly improve* your present level of initiative, circle 5 or 6.
- If you are a real self-starter but could still demonstrate *more* initiative, circle 7 or 8.
- If you rarely procrastinate and have a reputation as a doer with great follow-through, circle 9 or 10.

As you rate yourself, keep in mind that you will have a few weak areas in your profile that will demand action on your part. If you circle a 7 or higher on this scale, you are committing yourself to do something about discovered weaknesses. Are you willing to do this?

Self-inventory scale
Initiative

Low									High
1	2	3	4	5	6	• 7	8	9	10

PART 2
Constructing Your Profile

Steps to Take: Visualising Your Strengths and Weaknesses

Now that you have rated yourself in the 12 critical self-improvement areas, you can begin building your personal profile to gain a better perspective of your strengths and weaknesses.

1. Study the profile sheet on the next two pages. Notice the 12 categories at the top, the scale from 1 to 10 on the left, and the squares at the bottom with page numbers assigned.

2. Return to the exercises you completed and record the numbers (from 1 to 10) that you recorded.

3. On the left part of the scale, locate the level on the column that equals the number at the bottom. Place a dot at this point.

4. Connect the dots or fill in the bar graph and you have completed your profile.

Inventory profile sheet

	SELF-ESTEEM	LEVEL OF WELLNESS	COMMUNICATION	QUALITY OF RELATIONSHIPS	SENSE OF HUMOUR	ATTITUDE
HIGH 10						
9						
8						
7						
6						
5						
4						
3						
2						
LOW 1						
Rating						
Page numbers	17	22	26	31	36	42

ASSERTIVENESS	LEVEL OF JOB SKILLS	QUALITY OF PERFORMANCE	SELF-MANAGEMENT	CREATIVITY	DEGREE OF INITIATIVE		
						10	HIGH
						9	
						8	
						7	
						6	
						5	
						4	
						3	
						2	
						1	LOW
						Rating	
47	52	56	61	64	69	Page numbers	

Example
INVENTORY PROFILE SHEET
'Dan'

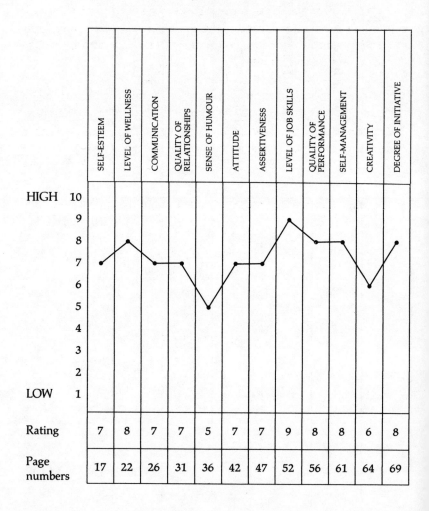

INTERPRETATION

- This profile suggests that Dan is highly conscientious, productive and dependable but takes himself too seriously in the work environment. As a result, seven categories – creativity, self-esteem, communication, relationships, attitude and assertiveness – suffer moderately.
- Humour is Dan's most critical weakness.
- Learning to laugh at the humorous side of work would have many benefits including: (1) better relationships with colleagues; (2) greater contribution to team spirit; and (3) more recognition from management.
- It is unusual to find a profile with such a low rating in the humour category and a good rating in attitude. There is normally a symbiotic relationship between humour and attitude – one contributing to the improvement of the other. This may be an indication that Dan has a good sense of humour but does not express it openly.

Example
INVENTORY PROFILE SHEET
'Beverly'

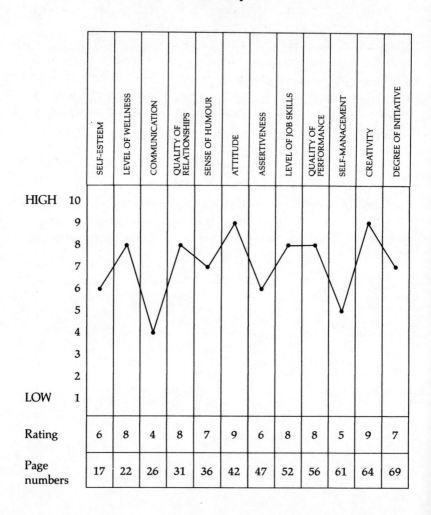

	SELF-ESTEEM	LEVEL OF WELLNESS	COMMUNICATION	QUALITY OF RELATIONSHIPS	SENSE OF HUMOUR	ATTITUDE	ASSERTIVENESS	LEVEL OF JOB SKILLS	QUALITY OF PERFORMANCE	SELF-MANAGEMENT	CREATIVITY	DEGREE OF INITIATIVE
Rating	6	8	4	8	7	9	6	8	8	5	9	7
Page numbers	17	22	26	31	36	42	47	52	56	61	64	69

INTERPRETATION

- When a profile shows only one category below the 5 level, it is a safe bet that concentration to improve that area will pay Beverly substantial and immediate dividends.
- A study of Beverly's profile indicates that improvement in the communication category would improve all the remaining areas, especially self-esteem and assertiveness. If Beverly were to save the profile while she took a course in communication or public speaking, a second profile should show a measurable change for the better.
- A 1- or 2-point improvement in the self-esteem, self-management and assertiveness categories could contribute significantly to Beverley's career progress.

Example
INVENTORY PROFILE SHEET
'Pat'

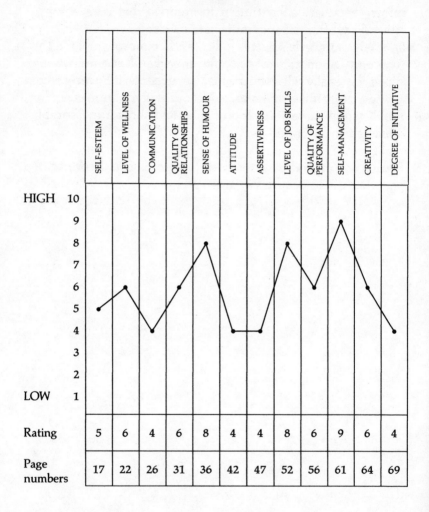

INTERPRETATION

- With three categories rated 8 or above and all others rated 6 or below (somewhat the reverse of most profiles) this may indicate that Pat was too hard in rating herself or is lacking in personal confidence.
- A high rating in humour with low ratings in communication, attitude, and assertiveness might be a signal that Pat enjoys a good sense of humour but does not share it with others.
- The 4 rating in initiative might indicate that Pat sometimes keeps busy with trivial matters while avoiding major challenges.
- The author suggests that Pat could show major improvements by concentrating on the four areas of low ratings (one area per week for four weeks) and then do a second profile for matching purposes.

PART 3
Interpreting Your Profile

Tips to Follow

What can you learn from your profile that will improve your personal life and career? Many discoveries are possible, provided you are open and honest with yourself and follow these tips:

Tip 1
Accept the fact that your profile is yours and yours *alone*. It reflects your personality, characteristics, strengths and weaknesses. It is not a scientific analysis, but puts you into a more favourable position to sense where you can make improvements. The more you study your profile, the more you will gain from it.

Tip 2
Often it is beneficial for you to compare your profile with those of others. Or to show and discuss your profile with another person you respect who can assist you in making your most valuable interpretation. To help you in making a comparison, an additional profile is provided on pages 86 and 87. Match any responses with your profile to see if there are any insights you can gain. Pay particular attention to the author's suggestions (interpretations) at the bottom of each profile.

Tip 3
Keep in mind that there is no such things as a perfect or 'model' profile. Among the 12 categories, we all have our weak areas. Most people who are honest with themselves have at least one column in their profile under 5. If none shows up, it may be an

Supplemental profile sheet

	SELF-ESTEEM	LEVEL OF WELLNESS	COMMUNICATION	QUALITY OF RELATIONSHIPS	SENSE OF HUMOUR	ATTITUDE
HIGH 10						
9						
8						
7						
6						
5						
4						
3						
2						
LOW 1						
Rating						
Page numbers	17	22	26	31	36	42

ASSERTIVENESS	LEVEL OF JOB SKILLS	QUALITY OF PERFORMANCE	SELF-MANAGEMENT	CREATIVITY	DEGREE OF INITIATIVE	
						10 HIGH
						9
						8
						7
						6
						5
						4
						3
						2
						1 LOW
						Rating
47	52	56	61	64	69	Page numbers

indication that the individual is blind to a weakness that is obvious to others.

Tip 4

A balance between weak and strong areas is often noticeable. For example, an individual may show a 9 or 10 in three areas and a 4 or under in a like number of areas. This is a healthy sign because the very fact that the individual has exceptionally strong areas indicates that the weak areas discovered can be raised. The number one benefit of doing a profile is to discover a weak area where immediate improvement can be made. It is possible for a person to have 7 or 8 very high categories only to have one or two extremely weak areas that are holding the person back from making the career progress that would otherwise occur.

Tip 5

A single area with a score under 5 can have a negative influence on the remaining 11 areas. For example, a low score in *initiative* (being a procrastinator) could delay or neutralise the positive effects of other areas. All 12 categories are interdependent which means that one very weak area can 'pull down' one's effectiveness in all others.

Tip 6

By the same token, a very high rating on one or more categories could 'pull up' the effectiveness of the individual in other areas. For example, a person who rates high in *attitude* and *sense of humour* probably does better in the *communication* category than would otherwise be the case.

Tip 7

One should keep in mind that a high score in one area does not necessarily 'cover up' the weakness in another area. For example, lack of job competence (*skill category*) will eventually surface even if the individual has a great *attitude* and *sense of humour*.

Tip 8
Share results selectively with others – especially superiors and career guidance professionals – so that additional insights may be gained.

Tip 9
Build a new profile every few months. If you use a personal computer, put your first profile into storage and add new ones for comparison purposes. This will help you to track your progress.

Tip 10
Lend your book and inventory to colleagues and friends to help them when they are going through down periods. Or present them with a book of their own.

Tip 11
Build your own self-help library. More and more ambitious career people are turning to self-help programmes to maintain their motivation. You can start your library by selecting from the titles shown on page 90, or order others listed in the back of this book.

Tip 12
When necessary, see a professional. As far as most categories are concerned, improvement remains a do-it-yourself challenge. This does not imply, however, that professional assistance should be avoided. Just the opposite. When the battery in your car runs down, a recharge is the first possibility. But sometimes a new generator, cable or battery is the solution. When personal problems are critical, seeing a professional counsellor and possibly joining a support group can be a wise choice. This is especially true in the field of mental health.

Improving neglected areas
Some Kogan Page titles which refer to profile categories are listed overleaf. Check your weak categories and consider reading more to start your personal improvement programme.

Profile category	Title
Self-esteem	*Developing Self-Esteem*, Connie Palladino
Wellness	*Fit for Work*, Scott W Donkin
Communication	*How to Communicate Effectively*, Bert Decker *Improve Your Concentration!* Sam Horn
Attitude	*How to Develop a Positive Attitude*, Elwood N Chapman
Assertiveness	*Assert Yourself*, Robert Sharpe *How to Develop Assertiveness*, Sam R Lloyd
Quality	*Quality at Work*, Diane Bone and Rick Griggs
Self-management	*Successful Self-Management*, Paul R Timm
Creativity	*Creative Thinking in Business*, Carol Kinsey Goman

A full list is available from the publisher.

Fill in this chart after reading page 91.

Weekly self-improvement schedule

Week 1. _____
(category)

Week 2. _____
(category)

Week 3. _____
(category)

Week 4. _____
(category)

Devote a Week to Improving Each of Your Weak Areas

A weak area is one that is 4 or more points below your strongest category. It is one where improvement is indicated and where results can be achieved and noticed by management. A primary purpose of the profile you have completed is to discover your weak areas.

Experience shows that for most people:

- Trying to improve in too many areas at the same time results in confusion and lack of motivation to continue.
- Concentrating on a single area (humour, assertiveness, etc) for a period of one week produces the best results.

If the week-at-a-time idea fits into your way of thinking, you may wish to complete the chart opposite and hang it where it can act as a reminder. Start with your weakest area and continue until you have brought all categories that are weak to a more satisfactory level.

Suggested Answers to Cases

Case 1 (Jill)
One possibility would be to sit down with Jill for at least an hour, and together work out a list of action steps that could help her to push her self-esteem higher. Such steps could include: (1) helping Jill to improve her physical image through an 'investment' in grooming; (2) assisting her to have and keep more social contacts; (3) getting her to 'open up' and talk more to others on a wide variety of subjects. (One good way to do this is teach her the art of asking questions.); (4) having Jill talk to her supervisor about steps she could take to make her more promotable; (5) giving Jill as many compliments as possible to help her build higher self-esteem; (6) recommending she take a course in public speaking.

Case 2 (James)
It would appear that James is afraid to move out of the protective shell he has built around himself. He needs to mix with others on a more open basis so he will receive the compliments he deserves. Joining a health club or engaging in some other non-work activity with colleagues might help. As a friend, you need to actually get him started in some fun activities where he can mix with others.

Case 3 (Gemma)
She may need help in understanding that gaining and losing weight regularly is detrimental to her overall wellness. Consistency in exercise and diet seems to evade Gemma. Perhaps the next time she comes close to a recommended weight, she can

learn to refrain from getting so excited over her new image that she forgets her weight programme. Gemma is paying a very high price for her lack of discipline. Also suggest that she talk it over with her doctor.

Case 4 (Keith)
Depending upon the quality and strength of the relationship between them, Maggie might consider one or all of the following: (1) read a good book on wellness and discuss appropriate passages with Keith; (2) ask Keith if she can accompany him when he takes his physical examination so the subject can be discussed with a professional; (3) introduce for discussion the impact his exhaustion is having on his career, family relationships and his long-term goals.

Case 5 (Charlie)
Although the supervisor should assume a good share of the responsibility, a major portion may belong to Charlie because he failed to keep communication lines open and let his emotional feelings dissipate. In short, Charlie allowed himself to be victimised by refusing to take action to restore the relationship or seeking a new career start elsewhere.

Case 6 (Melissa)
The supervisor needs to get through to Melissa that employees who are basically silent are always misunderstood. Open communication is required to be a good team member. Some small talk and laughter are necessary for most members to produce at an acceptable 'team' level. Perhaps the supervisor could make a practice of including Melissa more during internal sessions to give her the opportunity to 'open up' so others can get to know and support her.

Case 7 (Carole)
All working environments seem to have a few negative people. In Carole's case, the situation appears more severe. Even so, she should be able to raise a shield of positive thoughts so that she is not pulled down to their negative level. Perhaps she, the other

positive employees and the supervisor can devise and carry out a strategy to improve things. Most people learn to get along with negative colleagues or family members without it having a serious impact upon their mental health.

Case 8 (Trudy)
Yes, even when other candidates can be better in other areas, a sense of humour can make the final difference. Laughter created by a supervisor can bring a team closer together, strengthen other characteristics within the individual (especially attitude), and is a measure of good mental health. In general, a happy, relaxed departmental staff produces more and greater productivity and is the reason why Trudy was selected.

Case 9 (Shirley)
There is no evidence other than observation that this is possible. However, it seems logical that a negative view in one major part of life has a 'pull down' or 'draining' effect on another part. By the same token, a positive view in two or more environments can be mutually supportive and the individual could become even more positive in all other areas.

Case 10 (Kim)
If Alice does anything to help Kim it should be a very slow process so Kim does not lose her natural charm and effectiveness. In short, she should learn to assert herself slowly and in her own way. Kim could invite Alice to attend a seminar on assertive behaviour with her. They could then spend time analysing the behaviour of others who are non-assertive, assertive and aggressive so that Kim might see herself in a role where she would be most effective. Slowly, as she builds more confidence and understands western ways, Kim will find her own comfort zone as far as assertiveness is concerned.

Case 11 (Joanne)
It sounds as though Joanne had so much success when she first started being more assertive that it went to her head and she overstepped her natural limits. When the ill feelings she is

creating eventually come back to Joanne in full force, it is possible she will re-evaluate what has happened to her and learn to take a softer and more effective approach. In the meantime, her superior should initiate a series of counselling sessions to discuss the differences between assertive and aggressive behaviour and tell her directly the effect her behaviour is having on her colleagues.

Case 12 (Felicity)
No. Felicity is forgetting that as a supervisor, she will have the responsibility of training those in her department. This means she needs to know *more* about new computer hardware and software, not less. She will, however, be able to train one member of the team to train others so she can have more time for supervisory duties in the field of human relations and management. With a little more concentration on keeping her computer skills at a high level, Felicity might make an excellent supervisor.

Case 13 (Victor)
If you feel that you are a mentor for Victor, strategy 3 might be best and most convincing. This will have the added advantage of slowing him down a little in favour of quality to improve his relationship with you. The discussion might be best over lunch where there is less pressure andd Victor can express why he is in such a hurry to reach his goals.

Case 14 (Rita and Ralph)
The author prefers Ralph's plan because of the good feeling that occurs when one leaves an organised plan behind. For many, this approach enables people to relax more and dissipate normal stress. Either plan, however, can be effective.

Case 15 (Daisy)
Daisy is missing the point. If she applied the same techniques at home that she uses at work she would have even more free time and a happier lifestyle. For example, she would save time and money in the long run and improve the quality of her free time. Anyone as organised as Daisy in the work environment should

have plenty of energy left to have a more organised home life that would set her free to find greater personal fulfilment.

Case 16 (Jerry)

Jerry may be jumping the gun for two reasons. First, Ms North may actually be waiting for a winning idea. Second, Jerry may be overestimating his creative suggestions. In addition, it may be dangerous for Jerry to go over Ms North's head without a two-way discussion in advance. Of course, if her boss reacts in a humorous way to Jerry's written presentation, it could bring the attention he seeks. He should realise, of course, that his strategy carries a risk.

Case 17 (John)

It is doubtful. In all probability, the system would be just another idea that John would consider but never fulfil. Perhaps his problem is having a goal (marriage to a certain person, new home in a superior location, or to prove to a peer that he is more capable than the person thought) rather than a system. Most people need an emotional goal to make improvements, not just a system that will make it easier.